Nani and Jay Learn Finance

i want to be an

Entrepreneur

Written By
Evelyn Fernandez

DEDICATION

This book is dedicated to Ciahni and Jason. This series is inspired by you. I will never stop making everything I do about you. I've become a better person because of you and I love you more than words can express.

Jay came home from school one day and was very confused. His friend Julio told him that he will be a doctor when he grows up.

When Julio asked Jay what he wanted to be, he did not have an answer. He thought he would be a hero in the Army, just like his dad.

"Nani, Nani," Jay yelled, hoping his sister was not at choir practice. "OMG, what is all the shouting about Jay?" Asked his sister. "My friend Julio wants to be a doctor. Do you know what you want to be when you grow up?" He asks.

"Oh that is an easy question," said Nani, "an entrepreneur."
"An atrepe what," Jay never heard of this career before.
"Yes, I am already an entrepreneur." "Jay you didn't
know?" "No, I thought you had to be a grownup to have a
job," said Jay with a confused look on his face.

"Nope, that is the beauty of being an entrepreneur; you can be any age. An entrepreneur is a person that makes money for themselves using their skills. Follow me, let me show you something. I am 12 and I make my own money. "Really?" Asked Jay. He was so excited as he waited for his sister's response. "I make pictures to put up on walls and sell them to adults."

"Oh wait, huh what pictures," asked Jay. "You know I can draw right?" "Yes," he replied in excitement. "I draw stunning artwork, add some words on the bottom and put it in a frame. Then I sell it for five dollars. For example, I drew a flower with the words "Hello Sunshine" on the bottom, put it in a frame and sold it to mom.

"Oh," said Jay, "but how does this make you an entrepreneur?"
"Well, an entrepreneur is a person who works for themselves."
"Usually, adults work for somebody else. People have to ask for permission to stay home if they are sick, and all are working to make the boss rich, in return, the boss pays them a certain amount of money for every hour that they work.

"You see, most people go to college to learn a skill, then they use that skill and their time in exchange for money. An entrepreneur has a skill then uses it to start a business for themselves."

"One day, I saw that Mom went to the store, bought a frame with a picture of a flower, and hung it up on the bathroom wall. I asked Mom how much did she pay, and she said five dollars. I thought, hey, I want to make five dollars, and I know how to draw that flower," Nani continues to explain.

"I asked mom to take me to the dollar store, and I bought a frame. Then I drew a flower almost like the one mom purchased and put it in the frame, then asked mom if she would buy it from me, and she did. I paid one dollar for the frame, and I already had the drawing supplies, so when I sold it for five dollars and took away what I paid, I made four."

"You have four dollars?" asked Jay. "Well, I have more than that because I sold a lot of frames. You see, I don't have to ask anyone for permission for anything, and I don't have to go to work a set amount of hours.

"Since I love to draw, it doesn't feel like I am working. Plus I draw when I want to." Nani explains. "Then I sell the drawings and keep repeating it. That is an entrepreneur. When I grow up, I am going to sell houses because that makes you rich.

"Wow," said Jay, "I want to be an entrepreneur too. I want to make money using my skills and not have to go to work every day. Nani, when I grow up, I want to be just like you," said Jay. "Well, Jay, you can start right now. Remember, you don't have to wait to grow up to be an entrepreneur," said Nani. "Oh right, so what can I sell," he asked eagerly.

"You don't have to sell. You can do anything, like sing or dance at birthday parties, you can mow the lawn for the neighbors or rake up leaves."

"Wait, Dad showed me how to cut grass and trim the edges. How much do you think the neighbors will pay me for that?" asked Jay.

"Well, I'm pretty sure that you can get at least twenty dollars for that. You just have to ask dad if you can use his lawnmower". Jay shouts, "Oh man, that is awesome, I'm going to be rich, Dad, Dad, I need your help" as he runs to get his dad.

"Dad, can I borrow your lawnmower so I can mow the neighbors' yards and make money asked Jay?" "Sure Jay, but first, you have to knock on their doors and see if they want you to mow their lawn. Then you can tell them what you will charge and ask when they want it done."

Four of Jay's neighbors agree to pay him $20 each to mow the lawn this week, and he can come back every two weeks until winter.

"OMG! Nani Nani, look how much money I made this week," he shouts. "Wow, that is great, Jay. I am very proud of you. Now keep doing that and save your money in a jar like mine. You can do 20 or 30 yards per month when you grow up, and you would be working for yourself in your own business," said Nani.

By the time Jay was 21, he had so many yards to mow. He worked when he wanted to and kept all the money he earned for himself. Jay had become the Entrepreneur he said he would be.

About the Author

Evelyn Fernandez is a U.S. Army Veteran who holds a degree in Education. However, Evelyn has always been an entrepreneur. One of her many endeavors was having a business where she helped small companies improve their business credit and qualify for loans. She is the creator of a financial literacy set of flashcards and books for children inspired by her own. Her passion has always been to help others and what better way to do that, than by teaching something as valuable as personal finance.

As a first-generation Dominican immigrant, she came from poverty, but with her husband by her side became successful by applying good financial decisions. In her children's books, Evelyn teaches about budgeting, credit, debt, and investing. Evelyn believes that she can make a difference by continuing to spread the knowledge that is needed for children to grow.